A H-
and a

Written by
Stephen Rickard

RanS**m

The dog gets a hug.

The cat gets a hug and a kiss.

Can Pam hug a duck?

Can Kim hug a hen?

Is it a dog in a cup?

It **is** a dog in a cup!

Can I hug the dog in the cup?

Is it a cat in a mug?

It **is** a cat in a mug!

Can I kiss the cat in the mug?

Is it a rabbit
in a bucket?

Is it a rat
in a pot?

Can I hug the rabbit in the
bucket and the rat in the pot?